Jeffrey S. Turtletaub
32/322 Orrong Road
Caulfield North
Victoria
3161
61-466-475-097
mturtletaub@gmail.com

If I Am Not I – Recovering Your Ego
Managing Bipolar Depression

(The Secret to Flying)

By
Rabbi Jeffrey S. Turtletaub

Forward by Dr. Graeme Brazenor

Preface

✦ Preface ✦

For anyone who has sat in the dark and whispered, "I don't know who I am anymore."

This is not a book of advice.
It's not a blueprint.
It's not even a story, though it contains many.
This is a voice in the dark—a voice that says:
"You are not alone."
And perhaps even more powerfully:
"You are still here."

In a world overflowing with self-help slogans and curated wellness, *If I Am Not Me: Recovering Your Ego* dares to do something different. It tells the truth.

The truth about depression—not just as an illness, but as a gravitational pull away from the self.
The truth about mania—not just as a high, but as a flood of electricity that can both create and destroy.
The truth about healing—not as a destination, but as a daily return to your own presence.

Jeffrey S. Turtletaub writes not as an expert from the outside but as a fellow traveler from within.
He is not offering perfect recovery—he is offering **permission**:
- To stumble.
- To relapse.
- To revise your story.
- To keep walking anyway.

What you'll find in these pages is a rare kind of spiritual technology. A movement-based, breath-driven, Torah-infused path of reconnection

—with your mind, your body, and the core of your soul. A method that uses **walking** as ritual, **meditation** as medicine, and **truth-telling** as liberation.

You'll also find jokes. Memories. Tangents. Tears.
This book isn't polished like a TED Talk.
It's **alive**—like a real conversation with someone who loves you enough to tell it like it is.

If you're reading this in a hospital, on a bathroom floor, or at 3am when your thoughts won't stop—this book is for you.
If you've ever felt like a failure, a fraud, a broken thing—this book is for you.
If you've ever longed to come home to yourself but didn't know how—this book is for you.

And even if you never finish it, even if you only read one line and it helps you stay, or breathe, or smile—that's enough.

Because sometimes the secret to flying isn't found in soaring.
Sometimes it's just in **choosing to stand up, one more time.**
Hineni.
I am here.
And that, dear reader, is more than enough.

Forward By Dr. Graeme Brazenor (Neurosurgeon) M.B.B.S.(Hons), B.Med.Sci(Hons), F.R.A.C.S.

Jeff Turtletaub has done me the honour of asking me to write a foreword to his book.

I do so with great gravity, but also great joy. What I have read is a very precious (and short!) treatise
in which he tells us that we are not alone. -Even the concept brings me close to tears, and I am not
usually someone who sees himself as needing advice. Jeffe' mentions bipolar disorder frequently, but
his book is in no way restricted to folks with named diagnoses: it is for everyone in this terribly
troubled world.

I have many Jewish friends, thanks to the secondary school I was so fortunate to attend, and therefore
when I helped Jeff with his back problem I was attuned to see almost immediately that this man's
thinking was special. No matter what your religion

or upbringing, he has simple and powerful advice for you, to sample but a few diamonds:

You've been trying to fly. Gravity's been trying to hold you.
Superman isn;t relatable. A turtle, though— unbreakable.
This isn't a collection of essays. It's you, gathering your pieces.
Start where you are.
You don't have to climb the whole mountain.
Just move a toe.
The mountain will wait.
This method wasn't born in a lab.
I didn't learn it in a classroom or at a retreat.
I learned it on sidewalks.
On dirt trails.
In fogged-over mornings,
when my thoughts were spinning and the air felt too heavy to breathe.
And if you are about to email a strong message:
Write it down. Make tea. Dance in your room.

Record yourself if needed.

But don't send it yet. Don't hit publish. Don't leave the house.

God already wills you into existence.

But you must also will yourself into existence.

That's what gives your life meaning.

Mania doesn't define you.

Depression doesn't define you.

Even your trauma doesn't define you.

What defines you is what you do now.

What you choose next.

How you speak to yourself today.

My plea: read Jeffrey Turtletaub's humble but extraordinarily insightful offering, and discover that the power resides in you.

Graeme Brazenor F.R.A.C.S.[Neurosurgery]

Chapter One: Why This Book?

What This Book Offers
You won't find generic advice here. No magic formulas. No "12 steps to joy."

What you will find are tools and perspectives that helped me stay alive—and slowly become human again.

The Goal:
To help you gain real agency over your moods, habits, and story—without denying who you are.

The Tools:

- **CBT** – to interrupt looping thoughts

- **Meditative walking** – to reconnect mind and body

- **Aerobic movement** – to shift brain chemistry through breath and blood

- **Spiritual reflection** – for those asking deeper questions of meaning

These are grounded in a fusion of Maslow (needs) and Frankl (meaning):
Body first. Then mind. Then soul.

✦ STRUCTURE ✦

Part One — Body

(*Maslow: Physical grounding and survival*)

Short, clear chapters for when you're barely holding on. Designed to get you moving—mentally, physically, emotionally.

- **Chapter 1: Hotline & Crisis Note** – If you're in crisis, start here.

- **Chapter 2: Why This Book Exists** – Not a TED Talk. A note passed under the door.

- **Chapter 3: The Gravity Dialogue** – You've been trying to fly. Gravity's been trying to hold you.

Part Two — Mind

(*Frankl: Meaning, story, and reintegration*)

Longer chapters. Deeper reflections. Read when ready. This is where we rebuild identity and values.

- **Chapter 4: Why a Turtle?** – Superman isn't relatable. A turtle, though—unbreakable.

- **Chapter 5: The Great Gathering** – This isn't a collection of essays. It's you, gathering your pieces.

- **Chapter 6: If You Are in the Hospital** – The coffee is terrible, but the stories are gold.

- **Chapter 7: The Neurodivergence of the Bipolar** – Your brain isn't broken. It's running Cirque du Soleil.

- **Chapter 8: Spiritual Perspective & Free Will** – Your choices are sacred—even the small ones.

- **Chapter 9: Closing Reflections** – You are not your illness. You are your return.

A Word Before Reading:
Start where you are.
You don't have to climb the whole mountain.
Just move a toe.
The mountain will wait.

✦**HOTLINE & CRISIS NOTE** ✦

If ever you suspect you are near that line of crisis, when the pain overcomes your ability to cope, do the following right away:

Call someone. Anyone. You are not alone. If there is no-one to call and you won't go to the hospital on your own - find an all night McDonald's and just go buy yourself a soda. Do anything else. This feeling will pass. That decision is final.

- In Australia:
  Lifeline: 13 11 14
  Beyond Blue: 1300 22 4636
  Emergency: 000

- In the U.S.:
  988 Suicide & Crisis Lifeline
  Text HOME to 741741

But you *can* also go to your nearest hospital emergency room. You do not need permission. You do not need to explain everything right now. Just say: *"I need help."*

You matter. Even if it doesn't feel like it right now.

CHAPTER 2: WHY THIS BOOK EXISTS

(Not a TED Talk. A note passed under the door.)

This book is for people trying to cope with depression, mania—or both.

If that's you, I wrote this for you. Not for doctors, not for therapists, not for families (though they may benefit too). Just you.

I know how hard it is to focus when you're depressed or elevated.
I'll keep it short. I'll keep it clear. I'll keep it practical.

No One-Size-Fits-All

You are unique in your depression. There is no universal cure. No guaranteed fix that works every time for every person.

What helps one person might not help another.
What helps today might not work tomorrow.

The key is to find something that helps **today**—and work it.

This book isn't a cure-all. But it might help. It introduces a simple method I discovered that helps interrupt obsessive loops and depressive spirals. I call it a **"mind-in-body" method**—using **aerobic movement** to shift thought and emotion.

It's simple.
It's daily.
And for me, it brought relief.

My Type of Depression

I'm the kind of depressive who turns inward, obsessed with needing outside validation.
I didn't love myself. I was terrified of people.
My negative thoughts weren't just habits—they felt like instinct.

But they weren't mine. They were **imprinted**, not chosen. Still, I couldn't let them go.
Eventually, I wanted to get better. That's when everything began to change.

If you're suffering right now, I don't judge you.
I've been suicidal. I know the pull. I know the pain.
I hope something in these pages offers you **another option**.

What This Book Gives You

This book offers two core practices that helped me

manage depression—especially the kind rooted in identity, shame, and disconnection:

1. Movement-based mindfulness

By focusing attention on your body during aerobic movement—like walking—you interrupt the spiral of circular, negative thought patterns.

You shift from mental noise into embodied presence. That shift alone can bring relief.

2. Movement paired with spiritual mantra

For me, walking while meditating on a Mishna—a short ethical teaching from The Ethics of the Fathers, an aphorism from the Talmud —helped reconnect me to my identity, self-worth, and soul.

I'd repeat the Mishna aloud or silently as I walked. Slowly, its truth sank deeper into my being. It became not just a thought, but a felt experience.

Existential Depression Needs Existential Tools

The first approach—movement-based mindfulness—can help **anyone**.
The second—movement plus spiritual contemplation—may resonate most with those whose depression feels

existential, **spiritual**, or **rooted in identity loss**.

Whether your pain is biochemical, relational, or spiritual,
Whether you're feeling numb or overwhelmed,
Whether you're barely holding on or slowly getting better—

I hope something in this book helps lift the weight, clear the fog, or light the path forward.

Even if only a little.

Even if only for today.

CHAPTER 3: THE GRAVITY DIALOGUE

Walking as Neuro-Sculpture, Soul Retrieval, and Self-Repair

What if walking could heal you?

What if every step could loosen the old, tangled knots of thought?
What if posture wasn't just physical—but emotional, even existential?

What if the path to healing wasn't upward—but inward?
Downward.
Into gravity.
Into sensation.
Into breath.

A New Kind of Movement Practice

This book offers a method for transformation.
A synthesis of walking, awareness, and wisdom drawn from:

- **Jewish thought** (especially Jewish ethics and mysticism)

- **Modern neuroscience**
- **Somatic practices**
- **Lived human struggle**

It integrates:

- **Feldenkrais Method** – Gentle awareness of movement to unlock neuroplasticity
- **Alexander Technique** – Conscious inhibition of harmful patterns and subtle redirection
- **Ideokinesis** – Aligning posture with imagery and gravity
- **Body-Mind Centering** – Listening to the wisdom of cells, breath, and internal rhythm
- **Cognitive Behavioral Therapy (CBT)** – Breaking thought loops through embodied attention

This is not theoretical.
It is physical.
It is emotional.
It is lived.

It is not about self-improvement.
It is about self-retrieval.

This book does not ask you to run, to stretch, to sweat, or to achieve.

It asks only that you walk—with yourself—and listen closely to what you hear.

The Tortoise Shell and the Three-Second Rule

Two guiding images will appear often in this book: **the Tortoise Shell** and **the Three-Second Rule**.

These are not new inventions.
They are ancient ideas, re-articulated in a way that helps us cope with modern noise.

- The **Tortoise Shell** represents your **internal sanctuary**—a portable refuge of awareness and calm. You carry it everywhere. You can always return to it. It is yours.

- The **Three-Second Rule** is a simple practice: **pause for three seconds** before reacting. In that brief space, you give yourself time to return to the body, the breath, and the truth of who you are—before you speak or act.

These two ideas show up in many traditions:

- In **Jewish Ethics**: pause and choose the better

self

- In **Stoicism**: the gap between stimulus and response
- In **Zen**: presence over impulse
- In **neuroscience**: rewiring the default mode network through conscious interruption

In our distracted age—scrolling, reacting, performing—this wisdom is easy to forget.

But this walking practice is how we remember.

If It Was True in Thoreau's Time...

..."that most men lead lives of quiet desperation," how much truer is it now?

We are bombarded by input, yet starved for meaning. This method invites you to disconnect from the noise—and reconnect with the body, the breath, and the soul.

This isn't just about walking.
It's about **walking back to yourself.**

Depression, Identity, and the Return to the Body

This method wasn't born in a lab.

I didn't learn it in a classroom or at a retreat.

I learned it on sidewalks.
On dirt trails.
In fogged-over mornings,
when my thoughts were spinning and the air felt too heavy to breathe.

Here are the two insights that came from those walks:

1. Walking pulls attention into the body.

Aerobic movement lifts depression not just by "getting the blood moving"—but by anchoring awareness in **sensation**.

When you focus on walking—on your feet, your posture, your breath—
you pull yourself out of looping thoughts.
The nervous system calms. The critic quiets. A reset begins.

2. For some of us, depression is not just biochemical.

It's existential. It's spiritual.
It's a deficit of identity, meaning, or self-love.

For me, the breakthrough came when I paired walking with **a single, rhythmic mantra**:

the words of Hillel from Pirkei Avot:

"If I am not for myself, who will be for me?
And if I am only for myself, what am I?
And if not now, when?"

That mantra became my chant. My breath. My rhythm.

I didn't just repeat it. I **walked it**.
And it changed me.

✦ THE PRACTICE AT A GLANCE ✦

Walking as a Neuroplastic Ritual

Here's how to begin. You can add more over time, but this is the core:

1. Set the Frame *(CBT Layer)*

Ask yourself:

- What mental state am I in?

- What posture reflects that state?

- What new posture could support a better belief?

* * *

2. Awareness Through Movement *(Feldenkrais)*

Walk slowly at first. Observe without judgment:

- How does your body move?
- Where do you feel tension, collapse, or effort?
- What happens if you soften?

3. Inhibition and Direction *(Alexander Technique)*

Introduce a pause. Let the body reorient. Use gentle internal cues:

- "Let the head lead."
- "Allow the spine to lengthen."
- "Let the back widen."

These aren't commands. They're invitations.

4. Imagery Alignment *(Ideokinesis)*

Use simple mental images:

- A plumb line dropping through your center
- A balloon lifting your crown

- Roots growing from your feet

These images cue the nervous system to realign itself.

5. Embodied Presence *(Body-Mind Centering)*

Soften awareness further:

- Let your **organs** breathe
- Let your **bones** walk you
- Ask: *What part of me already knows how to move with ease?*

6. Mantra and Meaning *(Wisdom + CBT)*

Recite a simple phrase—a saying, a line of poetry, a psalm.
Let it ride your steps and your breath.
Let it rewire the story you tell yourself.

✦ WHAT TO EXPECT ✦

This practice doesn't offer miracles.
It offers movement.

Over time—day by day—it becomes a ritual of healing:

- Emotional states shift
- Posture adapts
- Identity rebuilds
- Thought becomes breath
- And walking becomes sacred again

You're not walking to "get in shape."

You're walking to come home to yourself.

CHAPTER 4: WHY A TURTLE?

Superman isn't relatable. A turtle, though — unbreakable.

Let me tell you a secret: I don't want to be Superman.

Superman flies because he's from another planet. He doesn't have to try. He's invincible, magnetic, otherworldly. He's what we admire — but he's not what we are.

Me? I'm a turtle.

And honestly, I think that's better.

Turtles Don't Fly — They Endure

A turtle doesn't leap tall buildings. It doesn't shoot lasers.
But it **survives**.

It moves slowly. Carefully. Deliberately.
It carries its home on its back.
It lives a long, long time.

And when the world becomes too loud, too fast, or too dangerous —
it doesn't fight.

It simply **withdraws into itself** and waits until it's safe to reemerge.

Your Shell Is Not a Prison

Maybe you've been told you're too slow. Too sensitive. Too stuck.
Maybe your quietness was mistaken for weakness.
Or your gentleness confused with fragility.

But here's what I've learned:
That "shell" of yours—the thing you thought was shameful or awkward or strange—
might just be your greatest strength.

It protects your core.
It gives you time.
It helps you survive.

And in that protection, you can grow.

The World Is Not Built for Turtles

It's built for eagles, for stallions, for wolves.
For people who push hard, talk fast, and perform confidently.

But many of us aren't built that way.

We think deeply.
We feel everything.
We move through the world in slower, stranger rhythms.

We need refuge.
We need silence.
We need time.

Why a Turtle?

Because turtles don't **conquer** the world.
They **persist** through it.

And in a culture obsessed with speed and performance, persistence is a kind of rebellion.

Turtles outlive most of the creatures that outpace them.

They do it by withdrawing wisely, by conserving energy, by knowing their own rhythms.

Build Your Shell

This book will show you how to do the same.

To create a safe internal refuge—your own **tortoise shell**.
To move at your own pace.

To define healing not as "getting back to normal,"
but as **reclaiming your natural rhythm**.

You don't have to be fast.
You don't have to be impressive.
You just have to **keep going**.

✦ A Turtle Prayer ✦

Let me carry my shell proudly.
Let me move at the pace of truth.
Let me rest when the world storms.
Let me withdraw without shame.
Let me return when I'm ready.
Let me know that I am not broken—only slow, only unique, only me.

CHAPTER 5: THE GREAT GATHERING

This isn't a collection of essays. It's you, gathering your pieces.

This book may look like a collection of thoughts—short chapters, poetic fragments, practices and metaphors. But it's not just a book. It's a **gathering**.

And not just of ideas.
Of you.

Of your memories.
Your moods.
Your insights.
Your rhythms.
Your sacred contradictions.

We Are Made of Fragments

If you've lived through trauma, illness, mania, depression—or any intense emotional rupture—then you know this truth:

You lose pieces of yourself along the way.

- A part of you gets left behind in that breakup.

- Another part is buried in that hospital bed.
- One part is frozen in a childhood room.
- And another, burned out in a job that drained your soul.

We fracture.
We fragment.

But healing isn't about "going back" to who you used to be. That version of you never fully existed anyway.

Healing is about **gathering** what's real.
And bringing it all **home**.

What Is the Great Gathering?

For me, the Great Gathering is both literal and symbolic.

Literally, it's the act of pulling together decades of writing, music, dreams, memories, poems, lessons, and healing practices—and bringing them into one unified offering.

Symbolically, it's what this book is trying to help you do:
Gather the lost parts of yourself.
The scared child. The masked adult. The artist you

forgot. The body you abandoned.
The wisdom you thought was gone.

Not to glue them back together perfectly. But to **hold them in one space**.
Like a circle of chairs in a room. Each part of you gets a seat. Gets a voice.

Even the wounded ones. Especially the wounded ones.

You Don't Need to Be "Fixed"

The world will tell you that you're broken.
That your diagnosis defines you.
That healing means returning to a "normal" that never fit you anyway.

But here's another view:

You are not broken.
You are **gathering**.
And in that process, you are becoming whole.

The Great Gathering Is a Daily Practice

It doesn't happen all at once.

- It happens in morning walks where you breathe deeper than usual.

- In late-night journal entries when you write something surprising and true.
- In conversations where you speak without performing.
- In silence.
- In music.
- In movement.
- In choosing to stay alive one more day.

You're gathering every time you act from love instead of fear.

Every time you choose truth over performance.

Every time you return to your body. To your breath. To this moment.

What You're Holding Now

This book is not a manual.
It's a mirror.

It's not a ladder.
It's a **circle**.

A gathering.

A return.

To the you who was never lost—just scattered.

And we're going to gather those pieces together, one step at a time.

CHAPTER 6: IF YOU ARE IN THE HOSPITAL

The coffee is terrible. But the stories are gold.

If you're in the hospital right now—reading this on a borrowed tablet, on printer paper your sister brought you, or just in your head while staring at the ceiling—this chapter is for you.

And if you're not in a hospital but love someone who is, this chapter is for you too.

You Are Not Alone

My sister and I are close. Closer than almost anyone in my life. She has done more for my healing than any professional ever has. And still—**she doesn't know what it's like** to ride the bipolar roller coaster from the inside.

No one really does, unless they're on the ride themselves.

We try to describe it. We try to explain.
But most of the time, people don't hear us.
They hear the alarm bells instead:

Doctor!

Meds!
Hospital!
Fix it now!

Not our voice.
Not the pain underneath our words.
Not the meaning behind our behavior.

Awareness Is Everything

Recently, my sister watched a video I made—part funny, part serious—and genuinely enjoyed it. But she also heard me say:

"Of course I'm insane. I'd have to be insane not to know I'm insane."

She laughed, but she also understood:
I wasn't joking. I was manic—or at least elevated. But I also knew it.

That awareness is everything.

I didn't try to fight it. I didn't deny it. I didn't pretend I was "fine."
I asked:

- What brought this on?

- What can I do with this energy?

- What should I *absolutely not* do with it?

That kind of pause can save your life.

The Most Important Truth in This Book

If you remember **only one thing**, let it be this:

Depression and mania lie to you. Constantly.

Every thought that comes up during an episode is distorted.
But here's the key: those distortions are not malicious. They're desperate.

The depressed brain lies to you because it's trying to **understand the pain**.
The manic brain lies to you because it's trying to **save you from despair**.

- Depression says: *"You're worthless. Don't bother."*

- Mania says: *"You're a prophet. Send that message now."*

Neither is true.
Both are survival mechanisms.

* * *

What Can You Do?

You **flip the script**.

When **depression** says:

You're ugly. Stay inside. Nobody loves you.

You say:

Call a friend. Step outside. Feel the sun. Text someone. Smell a flower. Take a walk.

When **mania** says:

You're a genius. Post the video. Send the manifesto. Everyone must know.

You say:

Write it down. Make tea. Dance in your room. Record yourself if needed.
But **don't send it yet**. Don't hit publish. Don't leave the house.

Enter the Batcave

You don't need to suppress your manic energy. You just need a **place** for it.

I call it the **Batcave**. Your creative sanctuary.

When you're elevated, this is where you go to **play safely**.

In the Batcave, you can:

- Write poetry
- Jam on guitar
- Talk to your camera
- Paint something wild
- Dance like a maniac
- Laugh at your own brilliance

Just keep it **in** the cave.
Don't post. Don't text. Don't blow up your life.

Let the fire burn—but not down the house.

And when you're low? That same Batcave becomes a **shelter**—a place to recover, to rest, to move gently outward again.

- A text here.
- A walk there.
- A soft hello.

* * *

If You're Depressed: Go Out

If You're Manic: Go In

That's the rule of thumb.
It's simple. But it works.

You don't need to be perfect.
You just need to **respond wisely**.

Healing isn't about control—it's about *response*.
Not fixing the feeling, but flipping the script.

And most of all, it's about love.
Quiet, steady, boundary-honoring love that says:

"I see you. You are not your episode. You're you."

CHAPTER 7: THE NEURODIVERGENCE OF THE BIPOLAR

Your brain isn't broken. It's running Cirque du Soleil.

Most people have been taught the phrase *"chemical imbalance"* when it comes to depression or bipolar disorder.
It's a simple metaphor—but it isn't the full story.

Your brain isn't a broken engine.
It's a living ecosystem.
And bipolar disorder is not just about "too much" or "too little" of a single chemical.
It's about how an entire network misfires, overcorrects, and swings back.

What's Really Happening Chemically?

Bipolar disorder involves **cyclical dysregulation**—your brain overshoots and undershoots certain neurotransmitter levels and receptor sensitivities. Not just quantity, but *timing* and *sensitivity*.

Here are the three big players:

- **Dopamine** – motivation, pleasure, reward

- ↑ Excess in mania (impulsivity, euphoria, racing thoughts)
- ↓ Deficiency in depression (apathy, low drive)

- **Serotonin** – mood regulation, sleep, appetite
  - Often low in both mania and depression, but strongly linked to depression

- **Norepinephrine (noradrenaline)** – alertness, stress response
  - ↑ Elevated in mania
  - ↓ Decreased in depression

But it's not just the chemicals. It's the **receptors**, the **circuits**, the **sleep-wake rhythms**, the **stress response**, and even inflammation.

Bipolar disorder is bio-psycho-social:

- **Biological**: Genes, neurotransmitters, circadian rhythms
- **Psychological**: Trauma, thought patterns, coping style
- **Social**: Stress, isolation, lifestyle triggers

* * *

What Brain Imaging Shows

Functional MRI studies consistently reveal:

- **Hyperactivity in the amygdala** during mania (the emotion center runs hot)

- **Reduced activity in the prefrontal cortex** (decision-making and impulse control go offline)

- **Abnormal white matter connections** between brain regions (communication misfires)

This isn't a moral failing.
This is circuitry.

And yet—even here—you have power.

Why This Matters

Understanding the biology helps you understand the *why* behind your experience.
You're not "lazy" when depressed; your dopamine pathways are muted.
You're not "crazy" when manic; your stress and reward systems are overfiring.

This knowledge also helps you **plan your response**:

- **Medication** may be necessary.

- **Sleep hygiene** matters enormously.
- **Walking, movement, and ritual** calm the nervous system.
- **Boundaries** protect relationships during mood swings.

The science won't fix you on its own. But it will help you stop blaming yourself.

Cirque du Soleil, Not a Broken Ride

Think of your brain as Cirque du Soleil.

It's dazzling. It's creative. It's high-risk. It's constantly pushing the edge of what's possible.
But sometimes the acrobats slip, the timing collapses, the whole act falls into chaos.

That's not failure.
That's the cost of running a high-wire show.

With training, safety nets, and rehearsal, the same troupe can perform breathtaking feats again.

So can you.

The Takeaway

Your brain isn't broken.
It's sensitive, complex, and powerful.
But it needs structure.
It needs recovery.
It needs rituals that anchor it when the circus goes wild.

That's what the rest of this book is about:
Building those rituals.
Training your acrobats.
Creating a show that's sustainable, not just spectacular.

CHAPTER 8: SPIRITUAL PERSPECTIVE & FREE WILL

Your choices are sacred—even the small ones.

Let's be honest: When you're depressed—or manic—the idea of "free will" can feel like a joke.

You don't feel in control.
You don't feel like there's even a "you" present to make a decision.
You feel like a passenger in your own mind.

And yet…

You are still here.

Which means: at some point, on some level, you **chose** to stay.

That alone makes you powerful.

Free Will Isn't Constant—It's a Muscle

One of the most helpful teachings I've encountered is from Rabbi Eliyahu Dessler, who said:

"Free will exists at the point of struggle."

Not in the easy things.

Not in the automatic things.
But in the edge.

When the alarm goes off and you **want** to stay in bed but **could** get up…
When you want to text someone something cruel but **could** pause…
When you feel the pull of a relapse but **could** take a walk first…

That's the battle line.
That's where free will lives.

And like a muscle, it gets stronger with use.

Will Is the Path to Joy

Resilience is the product of will.

Without will, we can't experience real happiness—because happiness requires direction.
Not being pulled around by moods, but **choosing** where to aim your energy.

You don't need to control your brain chemistry to have free will.

You need to create **enough space** to make a small choice.

Then another.

Even one conscious breath is an act of agency.
Even brushing your teeth when you want to disappear is an act of rebellion.

Good and Evil Are Stability and Instability

Let me offer you a radical reframe.

The biblical word for evil is **"ra"** — but it doesn't just mean "bad" in the moral sense.
In its deeper usage, **ra means unstable**. Shaky. Unformed. Fragmented.

By contrast, **"tov"** — good — means complete, stable, solid.

So when you feel unstable, you are not evil.
You are **unformed**.

And when you move toward greater stability — through small, steady choices — you become more **good**. Not morally superior. Just more **you**.

The World Isn't a Test — It's a Lab

You are not here to earn points.
You are not here to pass a test.

You are here to grow, to try, to fall and rise again.

The spiritual view of free will is not about reward or punishment.
It's about participation.

God already wills you into existence.
But you must also will yourself into existence.
That's what gives your life meaning.

You Are Sacred Because You Can Choose

Even when you don't feel spiritual.
Even when you don't believe in anything.
Even when you're numb, ashamed, or lost—

You can choose to take one step.
You can choose to be thankful for your food.
You can choose to call someone.
You can choose to brush your teeth.
You can choose to not send the email.

That choice is holy.

Because it's a **return**—to yourself, to presence, to love.

And love is always God's native language.

CHAPTER 9: CLOSING REFLECTIONS

You are not your illness. You are your return.

Let's take a moment.

You've walked with me through depression, mania, neuroscience, movement, memory, prayer, family wounds, and the hidden architecture of the soul.

And now—here you are.

Still reading.
Still curious.
Still breathing.

That's everything.

You Are Not Your Diagnosis

You may have been told:

- You're bipolar.

- You're borderline.

- You're ADHD.

- You're broken.

- You're too much.
- You're not enough.

But none of that is your essence.

Those labels may help explain how your brain works.
They may guide medication, therapy, or support.
But they are **not your identity**.

They are the weather.
You are the sky.

Your Illness Is Not Your Identity

Mania doesn't define you.
Depression doesn't define you.
Even your trauma doesn't define you.

What defines you is what you do now.
What you choose next.
How you speak to yourself today.

Your power lies in your return.

- When you spiral, and then stand up again: that's you.
- When you relapse, then reach out: that's you.
- When you forget, then remember who you are:

that's you.

Every time you return to presence, to self-kindness, to your values—you reclaim your soul.

Healing Is Not Linear—It's Rhythmic

The journey isn't up a ladder. It's more like a spiral.

You'll revisit the same lessons. The same wounds.
But each time, a little wiser.
A little softer.
A little more honest.

You will fall. That's part of it.
You will get tired. That's natural.

But each time you come back, you are stronger—not just in wisdom, but in your strength of resilience and free-will.

Your Worth Is Unshakable

You don't have to earn love.
You don't have to prove your worth.
You don't have to be "better" to be valuable.

You are already a soul.

And your soul is a breath of God.

That never changes.

Even when your moods change.
Even when your thoughts betray you.
Even when you forget.

The Return Is the Point

This book began with pain.
It moved through practice, memory, metaphor, and myth.
But it ends here:

In the moment you choose to return.

Return to breath.
Return to your feet on the ground.
Return to your name, your rhythm, your truth.

Even if it's messy. Even if you're limping.
Even if your voice shakes.

Return anyway.

You are not your illness.
You are your return.

Epilogue/SOUL: THE SECRET TO FLYING

An Expanded Exploration of Hineni — "I Am Here"

The Power of Saying "I Am Here"

A Journey from Hiding to Holy Presence

Introduction: The Threshold Between Absence and Presence

There are moments—often many—when we stand at the threshold between who we have been and who we might become.

We hear our name—not called by a person, but by **existence itself**.

And we must choose:

- Hide or reveal.
- Absence or presence.
- The comfort of a smaller self…
- Or the terrifying possibility of our true magnitude.

In the Hebrew language, that response—when we step forward—is a single word:

Hineni
Here I am.

✦ Part 1: The Archaeology of Hiding — Understanding Ayeka ✦

"Where are you?" is not a location. It's a soul-check.

The First Question in the Bible

When Adam hides after eating from the Tree, God asks:

"Ayeka?"
"Where are you?"

God doesn't ask *what* Adam did.
God doesn't demand an explanation.
God just wants to know:

Where did **you** go?

Ayeka Is Not a Game of Hide-and-Seek

In Hebrew, the root **eykh** shows up in words like:

- **Eykhut** (quality)
- **Eykha** ("How lonely sits the city…")

So when God says *Ayeka*, it's not about GPS. It's about **essence**.

What is your state?
What have you become?
Where are you in relation to yourself?

We All Hide

We hide in many ways:

- Curated personas
- Perfectionism
- Rage
- Addiction
- Political certainty
- Intellectualism
- Spiritual bypassing

We even hide behind therapy.

* * *

Shame Drives Us Underground

Like Adam and Eve, we gain a kind of "knowledge" —
of good and evil, of complexity.
But we lack the inner strength to hold that awareness.

And so we hide.

We hide from others. From God.
But most of all, from **ourselves**.

Hiding Blocks the Very Thing That Heals Us

We cannot be loved for our true self if we won't reveal our true self.

The first movement of healing is not insight.

It's **presence**.

It's the courage to be seen.

Part 2: The Courage of Radical Presence — The Meaning of Hineni

Beyond "I'm here" to "Here I am."

The Difference Between "I'm Here" and "Hineni"

- "I'm here" = attendance
- "Hineni" = availability

When Abraham, Moses, Samuel, and Isaiah say "Hineni," they are saying:

"I am fully present—without knowing what's coming next."

That's faith.
That's vulnerability.
That's **power**.

The Yes Comes Before the Details

Moses still says: "I am slow of speech."
Isaiah still says: "My lips are impure."
Jeremiah still says: "I am but a child."

But they say it **after** Hineni.

Not instead of it.

Hineni Means: I Am Not Waiting to Be Worthy

You don't wait to be ready.
You show up **as you are**.

Hineni is not perfect faith.
Hineni is **radical availability**.

The Secret Is in the Becoming

God doesn't ask for perfection.
God asks for **presence**.

When you show up with your reality—however messy, scared, insecure—you become capable of transformation.

www.ingramcontent.com/pod-product-compliance
Lightning Source LLC
Chambersburg PA
CBHW060033040426
42333CB00042B/2435